D1493463

DINOWORLD

INCREDIBLE ENCOUNTERS WITH THE WORLD'S LOST DINOSAURS

ARCHIE BLACKWELL

CONTENTS

IMAGINE MY ASTONISHMENT when, several years ago, I discovered that my great grandfather Edward Blackwell had been a dinosaur fossil hunter in the American West. My father had recently died and I was startled to come across numerous journals hidden away in his dusty attic. They were the writings of Edward – a shock, for my father had never spoken of him and somehow I sensed that a dark and shameful secret surrounded his name.

Eagerly I examined the musty, yellowing pages and found they were crammed with vivid records of Edward's bone-hunting days in the 1870s and 1880s. This had been a time when the excitement of spectacular dinosaur discoveries gripped America, and Edward, a keen student, had found himself in the fortunate position of assisting the great fossil specialist Othniel Charles Marsh.

However, as I made my way through the notebooks, a disturbing picture emerged. For it seems that Edward's "hobby" had turned into an all-consuming passion. As he became more obsessed with the incredible creatures thrown up by the ancient rock layers, he took to spending weeks alone in the field. His journals record that he found an enormous, dagger-like tooth in Montana; instead of sharing his find with colleagues, he became consumed with the desire to uncover more fossils that would prove the tooth belonged to a truly colossal predator.

Amongst the clutter in my father's attic I came across personal letters from Edward's wife and doctors. These seemed to suggest that he had become seriously unstable. Scribbled entries in Edward's journals show that he was having dreadful dreams, visions where he found himself alone in a terrifying prehistoric world. He came to believe he had actually seen the monstrous dinosaur whose bones he was hunting and like a man possessed, spent every moment he could in search of further remains.

I set to finding out everything I could about my great grandfather – and I discovered that his story is a desperately sad one. As Edward's grip on reality loosened, he was eventually admitted to a lunatic asylum. Hospital reports chronicle his descent into madness, his crazed conviction that he had walked with dinosaurs. But, there is more. For one morning in the year of 1894, Edward escaped the restraints that shackled him and seemingly vanished into thin air. His tale was soon forgotten, covered up by his family who were anxious to hide the shame of his mental illness.

For the past few years I have been haunted by Edward's story and the mystery of his strange disappearance. This book is a tribute to my lost relative, and to the vanished world that gripped him so. Included are several excerpts from Edward's journals – not because these writings add scientific weight to the book, but because they date from a time when the discovery of previously unthought-of monsters shook the world.

Archie Blackwell
– BOULDER, COLORADO

What was this creature that stalked me? From behind the trees I heard footfalls. Leaves rustled, a stick snapped, but the forest was otherwise still. As I strained to see in the gloomy half-light, I was suddenly aware that two glinting eyes had fixed upon me. And then a low and terrifying snarl filled the air and pointed fangs flashed in the shadows — truly, it seemed I was staring into the jaws of death . . .

AN EXTRACT FROM EDWARD BLACKWELL'S JOURNAL,
DATED 6 JULY 1892

LOST WORLD

Perhaps I dreamed, for it seemed I found myself at the heart of a lost world. Though I could not have known it, Earth seemed vast and untouched, a wild and savage place without man or civilization. Strange vegetation grew all around, ferns and thick groves of palm-like trees. Startled by a slow flapping noise, I looked up to see a creature such as I'd never seen before. Far larger than any bird, it had curious bat-like wings and sharp, little teeth glinting in a long jaw. And then suddenly I became aware of a distant thudding noise. Fearfully I crouched and listened – and the boom of pounding steps steadily increased in volume until the very ground began to shudder beneath my feet...

AN EXTRACT FROM EDWARD BLACKWELL'S JOURNAL,
DATED 4 DECEMBER 1889

6

RULERS of the EARTH

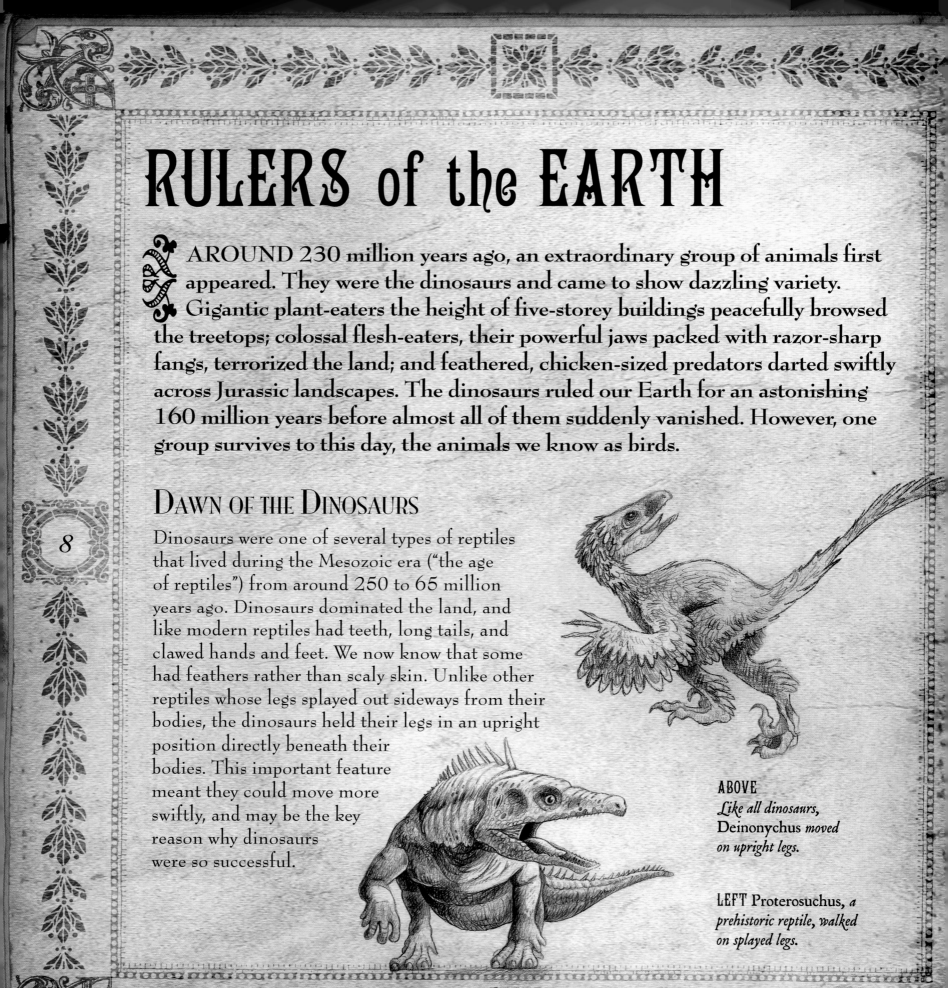

AROUND 230 million years ago, an extraordinary group of animals first appeared. They were the dinosaurs and came to show dazzling variety. Gigantic plant-eaters the height of five-storey buildings peacefully browsed the treetops; colossal flesh-eaters, their powerful jaws packed with razor-sharp fangs, terrorized the land; and feathered, chicken-sized predators darted swiftly across Jurassic landscapes. The dinosaurs ruled our Earth for an astonishing 160 million years before almost all of them suddenly vanished. However, one group survives to this day, the animals we know as birds.

DAWN OF THE DINOSAURS

Dinosaurs were one of several types of reptiles that lived during the Mesozoic era ("the age of reptiles") from around 250 to 65 million years ago. Dinosaurs dominated the land, and like modern reptiles had teeth, long tails, and clawed hands and feet. We now know that some had feathers rather than scaly skin. Unlike other reptiles whose legs splayed out sideways from their bodies, the dinosaurs held their legs in an upright position directly beneath their bodies. This important feature meant they could move more swiftly, and may be the key reason why dinosaurs were so successful.

ABOVE
Like all dinosaurs, Deinonychus *moved on upright legs.*

LEFT Proterosuchus, *a prehistoric reptile, walked on splayed legs.*

LIVING DINOSAURS

Most scientists now agree that birds evolved from small, flesh-eating dinosaurs. In 1861, a remarkable fossil was uncovered in a German quarry, revealing a Jurassic creature known as *Archaeopteryx* ("ancient wing"). Often credited as being the first bird, *Archaeopteryx* had feathers for flying, a beak and bird-like feet. However it also had dinosaur features such as teeth, fingers and claws.

In 1996 Chinese scientists discovered *Sinosauropteryx* ("Chinese reptilian wing"), a dinosaur that had a downy covering on its body. Further exciting finds have proved that some dinosaurs such as the vicious meat-eater *Velociraptor* ("swift thief") had feathers. Early feather-like structures were probably used for keeping the body warm, while feathers for display and flight developed later.

RIGHT Archaeopteryx *is the earlist bird in the fossil record.*

ABOVE *Scientists now know that the fearsome little predator* Velociraptor *had feathers.*

RIGHT Sinosauropteryx *was the first feathered dinosaur to be discovered.*

❧ BAROSAURUS ☙

A *Barosaurus* ("heavy lizard") herd ambles across
a plain in what is now North America. These
enormous dinosaurs from the late Jurassic period
reached up to 28 m in length and were closely
related to the better known *Diplodocus*.

Their fantastically long necks allowed them
to reach high into trees for feeding, while their
powerful, whip-like tails were probably used
to warn off predators.

DINOSAUR PLANET

IMAGINE Earth during the Triassic period, 230 million years ago. The climate is much hotter than today, and vast deserts and strange vegetation cover the planet's surface. There are no flowers or grass. Instead of there being five continents, the world consists of one huge landmass called Pangaea ("all earth"), surrounded by a single giant ocean, Panthalassa ("all sea"). *Eoraptor* ("dawn thief") is one of the earliest known dinosaurs – this fox-sized creature stalks the land on two legs, seizing lizards and other small prey with grasping hands.

ABOVE Eoraptor *was one of the first dinosaurs ever to walk the Earth.*

BELOW *The three periods of the Mesozoic era (250–65 million years ago).*

Triassic Period	Jurassic Period	Cretaceous Period
250–199 MILLION YEARS AGO	199–145 MILLION YEARS AGO	145–65 MILLION YEARS AGO

Changing World

Towards the end of the Triassic period, Pangaea began to break up. Over millions of years, the continents drifted apart, gradually forming the lands we know today. As the climate changed, so too did the dinosaurs' landscape. During the Triassic period, ferns, cycads and ginkgo trees covered the Earth. Later, during the Jurassic period, huge forests of conifer trees sprung up in dry areas and groves of cycads grew near water. Flowering plants first appeared during the Cretaceous period, and were soon the main form of plant-life.

13

ABOVE *Over time, Pangaea broke up and formed the continents as we know them today.*

LEFT *Fossils of Triassic ferns (far left) and ginkgo leaves (middle), compared with a modern ginkgo leaf (right).*

❧ SPINOSAURUS ❧

Possibly the largest predator ever to walk
the Earth, *Spinosaurus* ("spine lizard") lived
in what is now North Africa, and spent its
time in or near water hunting fish. With
long, crocodile-like jaws, its spiky teeth were
perfect for skewering slippery prey, though
it was big enough to have preyed on
smaller dinosaurs too.

The large sail on its back was probably used to
control its body temperature, and as a means of
attracting a mate in the breeding season.

SHARED WORLD

ALTHOUGH dinosaurs were the dominant land creatures during the Mesozoic era, they shared Earth with many other creatures. Some are true survivors – turtles and crocodiles first appeared during the Triassic period, while the earliest sharks date back to over 420 million years ago! Monstrous, now-extinct reptiles ruled the seas, while strange winged predators know as pterosaurs soared above the dinosaurs.

ABOVE Pterodactylus ("winged finger") was the first pterosaur ever discovered.

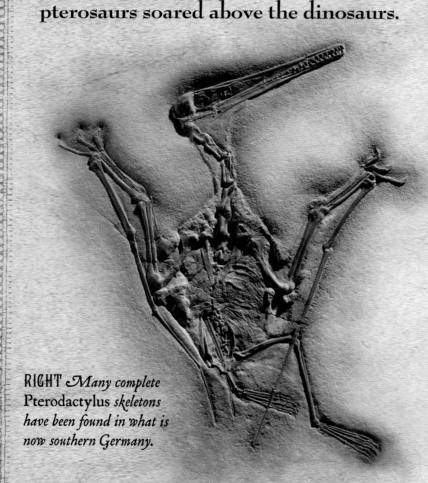

RIGHT *Many complete* Pterodactylus *skeletons have been found in what is now southern Germany.*

WINGED LIZARDS

The pterosaurs ("winged lizards") were flying reptiles with bat-like wings. Closely related to the dinosaurs, they showed huge variations in size – some, like the Jurassic *Anurognathus* ("without tail and jaw"), were just sparrow-sized, while others were the size of a small plane. The mighty *Quetzalcoatlus*, (named after the Aztec god, Quetzalcoatl) glided through late Cretaceous skies on wings measuring an incredible 11 m across.

The pterosaurs had light, hollow bones and leathery wings that stretched between their elongated fourth fingers and the sides of the body. Most were fish-eaters, though some may have preyed on insects or dead animals. Towards the end of their reign, only the larger pterosaurs remained as early birds competed with them for mastery of the skies.

16

DEADLY JAWS OF THE DEEP

Beneath the waves of ancient seas lurked some truly terrifying reptiles. The late-Cretaceous *Mosasaurus* ("lizard of the Meuse River") was one of the deadliest hunters of prehistoric waters. Fifteen metres in length, this crocodile-like predator swam by slowly winding its long body from side to side, but could swiftly accelerate to ambush its victims with horribly savage jaws. *Liopleurodon* ("smooth-sided teeth") was a huge predator with a large head and short neck. Using its four paddle-like limbs to cruise silently through middle-Jurassic seas, this creature had immense, powerful jaws to drive rows of razor-sharp teeth into its prey.

BELOW Liopleurodon *clamps powerful jaws around its victim.*

17

"The plesiosaurus has the head of a lizard, the teeth of a crocodile, the neck has forty-one vertebrae and resembles the body of a serpent ... the ribs of a chameleon, and the paddles of a whale."
RICHARD OWEN, FOSSIL SPECIALIST, DESCRIBING PLESIOSAURUS IN 1840

RICHARD OWEN

⊱ LIOPLEURODON ⊰

The deadly *Liopleurodon* feasts on an *Ophthalmosaurus*, a dolphin-like marine reptile from the late Jurassic period. *Liopleurodon* reached lengths of 10 m and was larger than today's killer whale. Incredibly successful, this monstrous predator terrorized prehistoric seas for close to 10 million years.

FOSSIL FINDS

WITHOUT fossils we would know nothing about dinosaurs or the incredible creatures that shared their world. Most dinosaurs rotted or were eroded away without a trace, and only a tiny proportion became fossilized. As well as fossils of bones, teeth and claws — and very rarely soft parts such as skin — trace fossils such as footprints and teeth marks provide vital clues about dinosaurs and their way of life.

ABOVE *A coprolite, or dinosaur dropping, gives vital clues as to what dinosaurs ate.*

DINOSAUR DETECTIVES

After bone fossils have been carefully excavated, the challenge of placing them together begins. Whole skeletons are a rare find, and fossil specialists (palaeontologists) carry out much detective work in order to piece together jumbled bones. They need to work out how a dinosaur stood and carried its weight. Engineering tests on models help with this — for example, the tail needs to counterbalance the head and neck.

LEFT *Palaeontologists painstakingly work together to extract a huge dinosaur fossil from a rockface.*

WINDOWS ON A LOST WORLD

Bone fossils reveal what dinosaurs looked like but trace fossils tell us about how these creatures behaved. Footprints can show whether a dinosaur walked on two feet or four, whether it was part of a group, and how fast it was moving. Droppings, or coprolites, can reveal what dinosaurs ate. An enormous coprolite, thought to belong to a *Tyrannosaurus rex* ("tyrant king"), was discovered in Canada in 1998. It contained what appeared to be fragments of bone from the head frill of a young *Triceratops*.

ABOVE *This skeleton is that of Claosaurus ("broken lizard") – the name refers to the jumbled position of the fossils when first discovered in 1872.*

BELOW *Fossils form when water and minerals seep into the ancient layers of sediment covering an animal's dead body, turning it to rock.*

HOW FOSSILS FORM

Once an animal dies, soft tissues quickly start to rot away but hard parts such as bones and teeth last much longer. In order for these to be fossilized, they must be quickly covered by sediments such as sand or mud. In time, more and more sediment layers settle on the dead animal. Over millions of years, water and minerals seeping into the layers and once-living remains turn them to rock.

21

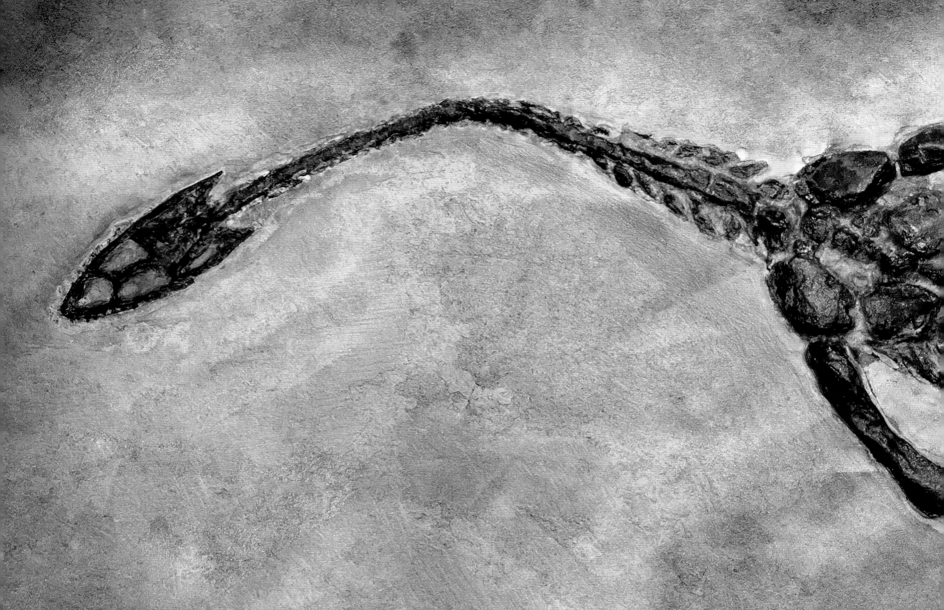

◈ PACHYPLEUROSAURUS ◈

Pachypleurosaurus ("thick-rib lizard") was a marine reptile that lived during the middle Triassic period in what is now Switzerland and Italy. With a long, muscular body, a thin neck and a tiny head, this small reptile (30–40 cm in length) used its limbs as paddles, darting through shallow water in search of shellfish. Several specimens have been found in Monte San Giorgio in Switzerland, a rich source of fossilized creatures from the Triassic period.

The FIRST DINOSAUR FIND

ABOVE *A rock hammer, vital to any fossil hunter.*

FAR RIGHT *Callipers can be used to measure fossils.*

BELOW *The lower jaw of* Megalosaurus, *first described by William Buckland in 1824.*

IT IS LIKELY that people have been finding dinosaur bones for thousands of years. Ancient legends surrounding mythical creatures such as dragons may well be connected to dinosaur fossil finds. However it was not until 1824 that William Buckland scientifically described the first dinosaur from an enormous fanged jawbone and other remains – this was the Jurassic predator *Megalosaurus* ("giant lizard"). In 1842, Richard Owen introduced the term dinosaur ("terrible lizard") to cover a group of large extinct reptiles.

"These stories look like fables, but I ask not your indulgence to believe them. There the monsters are, and I challenge your incredulity in the face of the specimens before your eyes; disbelieve them if you can."

WILLIAM BUCKLAND, PALAEONTOLOGIST, DESCRIBING MEGALOSAURUS IN 1824

⁂ WILLIAM BUCKLAND ⁂

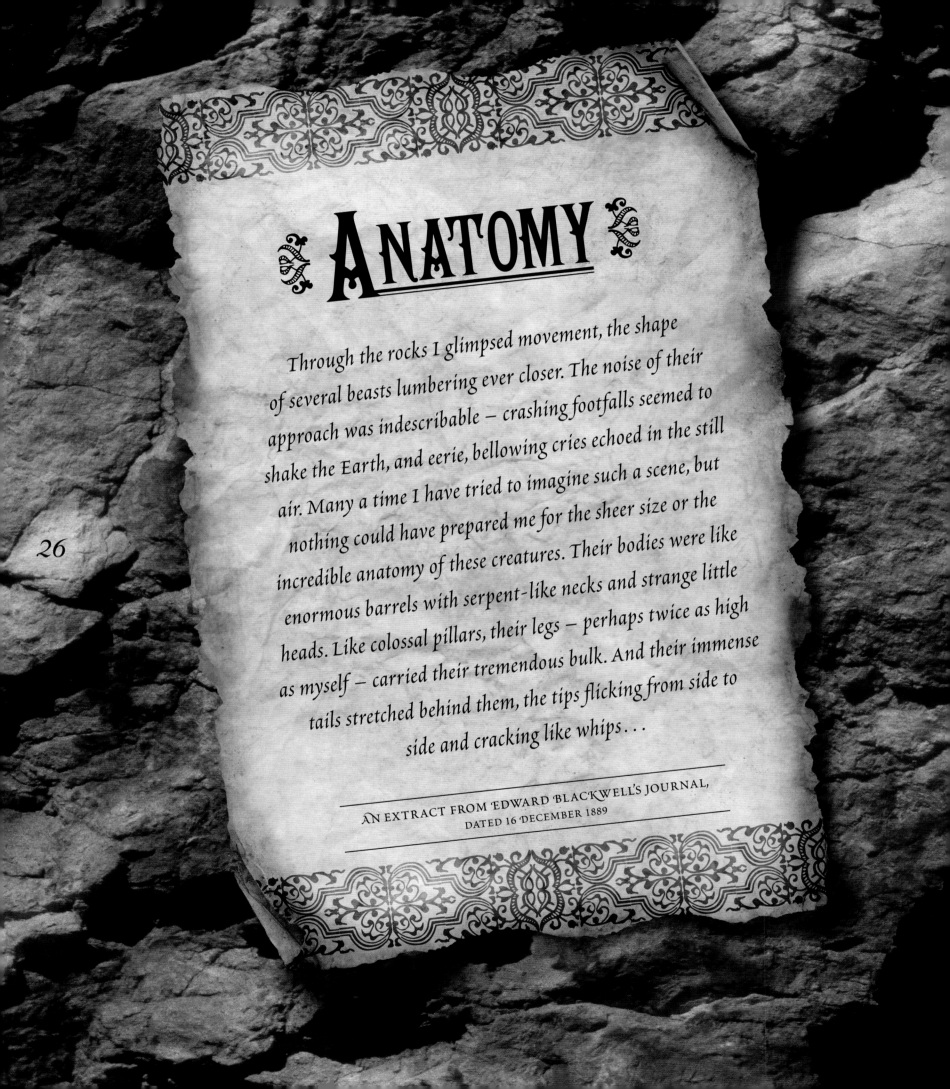

ANATOMY

Through the rocks I glimpsed movement, the shape of several beasts lumbering ever closer. The noise of their approach was indescribable — crashing footfalls seemed to shake the Earth, and eerie, bellowing cries echoed in the still air. Many a time I have tried to imagine such a scene, but nothing could have prepared me for the sheer size or the incredible anatomy of these creatures. Their bodies were like enormous barrels with serpent-like necks and strange little heads. Like colossal pillars, their legs — perhaps twice as high as myself — carried their tremendous bulk. And their immense tails stretched behind them, the tips flicking from side to side and cracking like whips...

AN EXTRACT FROM EDWARD BLACKWELL'S JOURNAL, DATED 16 DECEMBER 1889

A QUESTION of SIZE

BELOW Argentinosaurus *would have towered over almost all other dinosaurs.*

ALTHOUGH dinosaurs came in a startling range of sizes, it is beyond doubt that some were truly colossal — the huge sauropods were longer, taller and heavier than any creature that has walked the Earth since.

At around 80 tonnes — the weight of 14 bull elephants — *Argentinosaurus* ("Argentina lizard") is one of the largest dinosaurs that scientists can be sure of. However, tantalizing fossil finds offer the possibility of even bigger creatures. Only one vertebra bone of *Amphicoelias* ("doubly hollow") was ever discovered — and then lost again — but some have calculated this colossus may have weighed as much as 25 elephants!

BELOW *The range of dinosaur sizes, compared to humans.*

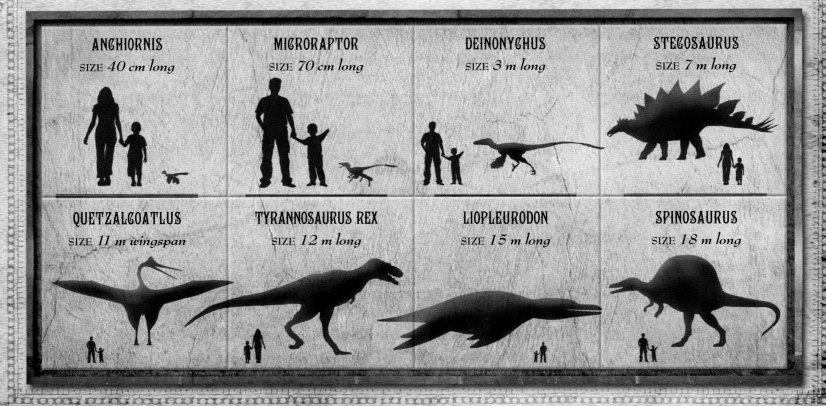

ANCHIORNIS
SIZE *40 cm long*

MICRORAPTOR
SIZE *70 cm long*

DEINONYCHUS
SIZE *3 m long*

STEGOSAURUS
SIZE *7 m long*

QUETZALCOATLUS
SIZE *11 m wingspan*

TYRANNOSAURUS REX
SIZE *12 m long*

LIOPLEURODON
SIZE *15 m long*

SPINOSAURUS
SIZE *18 m long*

SMALL AND VICIOUS

At the other end of the scale was one of the smallest dinosaurs, the late-Jurassic *Compsognathus* ("pretty jaw"). While giant plant-eaters peacefully browsed the treetops, this nimble, chicken-sized hunter prowled the land. It grasped prey with clawed fingers, ripping them apart with sharp teeth or swallowing them whole. Smaller yet was *Microraptor* ("small thief"), a crow-sized dinosaur from the early Cretaceous period. Although it couldn't fly, this winged creature had feathers and probably lived in trees, scrambling from branch to branch and feeding on small animals such as lizards.

ABOVE *A fossilized* Compsognathus, *with its sharp teeth and clawed feet clearly visible.*

RIGHT *The crow-sized* Microraptor, *one of the smallest known dinosaurs, was feathered but couldn't fly.*

BELOW *This tiny* Mussaurus *("mouse lizard") skeleton is actually that of an infant. A full-grown* Mussaurus *probably reached up to 3 m in length.*

29

CRYLOPHOSAURUS

Crylophosaurus ("frozen-crested lizard") lived in what is now Antarctica during the early Jurassic period. This impressive predator was over 6 m in length and had a strange and very unusual bony crest above its eyes. Not strong enough to use for fighting, the crest was probably for mating displays.

HEADS and HORNS

DINOSAURS came in all sorts of shapes and sizes, and many had bizarre projections of bone. The cow-sized heads of the huge plant-eaters were tiny compared to their enormous bodies, while the biggest skulls belonged to the much smaller horned dinosaurs. *Pentaceratops* ("five-horned face") had the largest head of any dinosaur. At 3 m long, much of it consisted of a bony frill extending over its back, probably used for display and defence. *Pachycephalosaurus* ("thick-headed lizard") had the thickest skull, with an extraordinary dome of solid bone. It was not strong enough for head-to-head combat with a rival male, but the dome could have been used to ram predators with brutal force.

INCREDIBLE CRESTS

Scientists have long puzzled over the strange and elaborate head crests that some dinosaurs sported. *Parasaurolophus* ("like Saurolophus") had a hollow, pipe-like crest on top of its skull. Many theories have been put forward as to its purpose – perhaps this dinosaur used it to push its way through undergrowth, or as a cooling device or for courtship displays. However, its most likely use was as a resonating chamber for making sounds. Low trumpet notes could have been sent out as signals about food and water, or to warn fellow dinosaurs of a lurking predator.

ABOVE *The mighty head of* Pentaceratops.

ABOVE *The impressive crest of* Parasaurolophus.

32

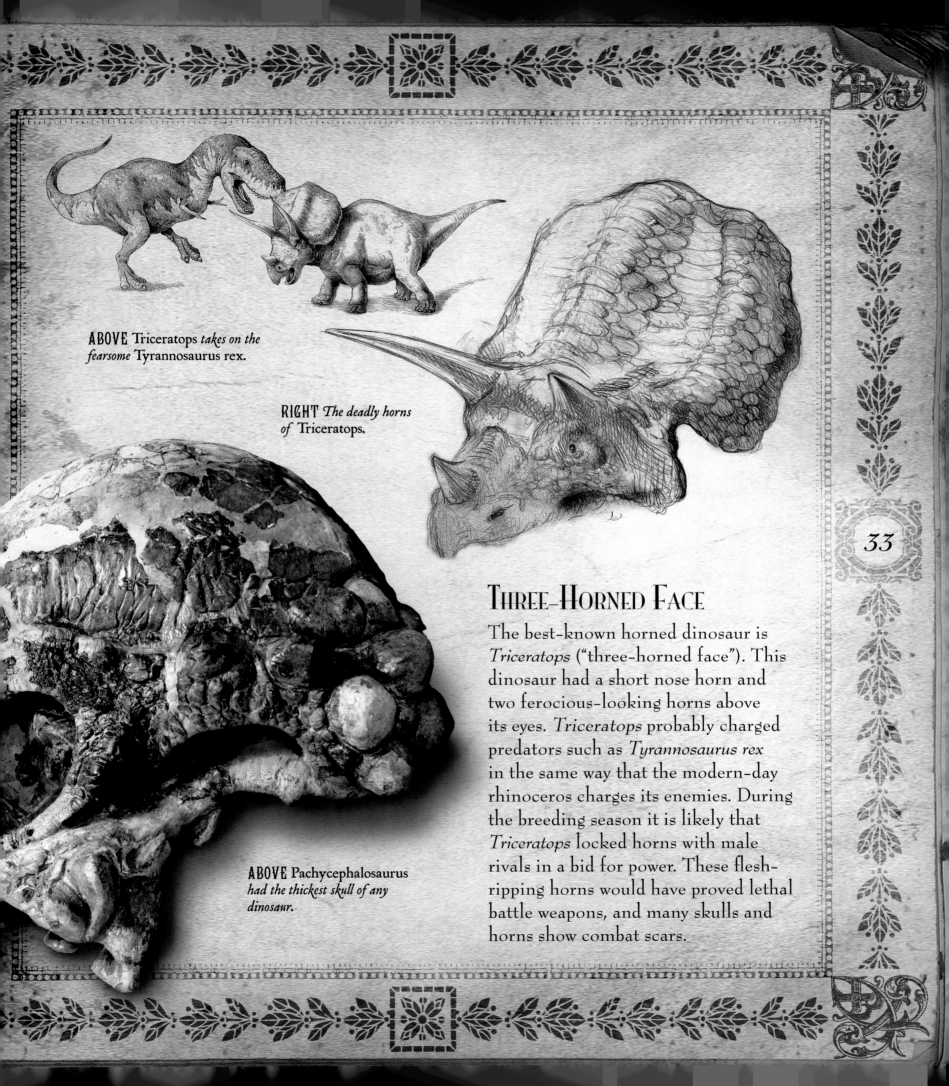

ABOVE Triceratops *takes on the fearsome* Tyrannosaurus rex.

RIGHT *The deadly horns of* Triceratops.

ABOVE Pachycephalosaurus *had the thickest skull of any dinosaur.*

THREE-HORNED FACE

The best-known horned dinosaur is *Triceratops* ("three-horned face"). This dinosaur had a short nose horn and two ferocious-looking horns above its eyes. *Triceratops* probably charged predators such as *Tyrannosaurus rex* in the same way that the modern-day rhinoceros charges its enemies. During the breeding season it is likely that *Triceratops* locked horns with male rivals in a bid for power. These flesh-ripping horns would have proved lethal battle weapons, and many skulls and horns show combat scars.

SKIN

In rare instances, preserved skin impressions are discovered alongside fossilized dinosaur bones.

These incredible finds reveal what the skin patterns of some dinosaurs were – for example, hadrosaurs had large reptilian scales, while armoured dinosaurs such as *Euoplocephalus* ("well armoured head") had protective, bony plates. Like the skin of reptiles today, dinosaur skin would have been tough, leathery and waterproof. We now know that many predators were feathered, and some had long, hair-like filaments. Even big dinosaurs known to have had scaly skin may have had patches of feathers or hair on parts of their bodies.

DINOSAURS IN COLOUR

The true colours of dinosaur species have long remained a mystery, but in 2010 scientists were able to reveal the actual colouring of a dinosaur for the first time. *Sinosauropteryx* ("Chinese winged lizard") was a small, feathered meat-eater that lived in China 125 million years ago. By examining the microscopic details of fossilized remains, the scientists discovered this creature had orange and reddish-brown feathers running along its head and back, and orange and white stripes on its tail. These striking feathers and colours were most likely there to attract a mate.

RIGHT *Edmontosaurus*

BELOW *Centrosaurus*

BELOW *Euoplocephalus*

LEFT *Polacanthus*

ABOVE *Corythosaurus*

ON the MOVE

THE meat-eating predators – and many of the swift-moving dinosaurs they chased – ran on their hind legs. The quickest dinosaurs had long, slim legs with shins longer than their thighs, and long, narrow feet. Their upper bodies tended to be lightly built with short arms. The slowest dinosaurs were the colossal, four-legged sauropods such as *Diplodocus*. Pillar-like legs supported their huge bulk as they ambled along, though – like elephants – they would have been capable of moving fairly quickly if they needed to.

ABOVE *The enormous front feet of* Apatosaurus *("deceptive lizard").*

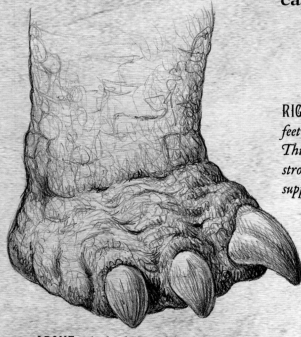

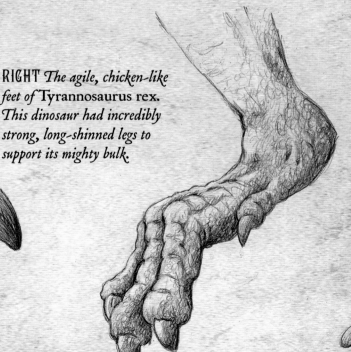

RIGHT *The agile, chicken-like feet of* Tyrannosaurus rex. *This dinosaur had incredibly strong, long-shinned legs to support its mighty bulk.*

ABOVE *The back feet of* Apatosaurus. *Like all sauropods, this dinosaur had massive, weight-bearing limbs.*

LEFT *The enormous back leg bones of* **Diplodocus.**

BUILT TO RUN

The fastest dinosaurs were most likely the ornithomimids ("ostrich mimics"). *Gallimimus* ("chicken mimic"), the largest of this group, was perhaps the quickest of all. A strange-looking creature with a long, bird-like head and a toothless beak, this dinosaur probably fed on plants as well as small animals and insects. It had athletic back legs and very long, slender foot bones. *Gallimimus* probably ran as fast as an ostrich with powerful, pounding strides. When pursued by a predator, speed was this dinosaur's main means of defence. Its long tail would have helped *Gallimimus* to stay balanced as it made sudden turns in a bid to escape death.

ABOVE *The long, toothless beak of* **Gallimimus.**

RIGHT *The ostrich-like* **Gallimimus** *was probably the swiftest dinosaur of all.*

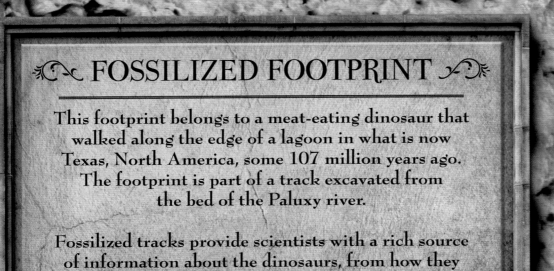

FOSSILIZED FOOTPRINT

This footprint belongs to a meat-eating dinosaur that walked along the edge of a lagoon in what is now Texas, North America, some 107 million years ago. The footprint is part of a track excavated from the bed of the Paluxy river.

Fossilized tracks provide scientists with a rich source of information about the dinosaurs, from how they moved to whether they lived in herds or not.

ABOVE The sickle-like talon of *Deinonychus*.

KILLER CLAWS

Claw fossils reveal much about their owner's way of life. Some dinosaur claws were blunt and harmless, useful for raking up plants or pawing the ground. Others were truly lethal weapons – narrow and dagger-sharp for slashing through flesh or hooked to pin down a struggling victim.

"TERRIBLE CLAW"

Deinonychus ("terrible claw") was a fast and vicious predator of the early Cretaceous period. This dinosaur got its name because of the huge, sickle-like talons on the second toes of its hind feet. Although there is some debate as to how the claws were used, it is most likely these flesh-ripping blades were flicked down to rip through a victim's skin and muscle. *Deinonychus* probably held down its prey with powerful hands and jaws, while a clawed foot was kicked out to slash the creature to death.

ABOVE The vicious claw of *Tyrannosaurus rex*.

RIGHT The enormous claw of *Therizinosaurus*.

SCISSOR HANDS

Therizinosaurus ("scythe lizard") was one of the strangest creatures ever to walk the Earth. With a small head, a long neck and a bulky body, its most distinctive feature was the three gigantic claws on its hands, the longest of which was an incredible 70 cm. The claws were too clumsy for attacking animals and therefore more likely used for raking up plants and pulling down branches. They may also have been used to frighten off predators such as the fearsome *Tarbosaurus*.

TERRIBLE TAILS

SOME dinosaurs were in possession of a truly terrifying weapon: a lethal tail. *Stegosaurus* ("roofed lizard") had four long spikes at the end of its tail, each around 70 cm in length. This dinosaur almost certainly used these spikes in defence, swinging its muscular tail to savagely strike out at predators such as *Allosaurus* . The tail of *Euoplocephalus* ("well-armoured head") ended in a massive bony club, 60 cm across. Swung sideways, this structure could be smashed into a predator's legs, crunching bones and bringing the creature to its knees.

BELOW Apatosaurus *may have flicked its incredibly long tail to produce a sudden cracking noise.*

42

CRACK OF A WHIP

The incredible, snaking tail of *Apatosaurus* is one of the longest known of any dinosaur. Some scientists believe that *Apatosaurus* and other sauropods used their long tails in defence, lashing out at predators with sharp blows. A sudden flick of the tail's tip would have produced a loud cracking noise, perhaps enough to deter predators from attacking.

BELOW *A shoulder spike from a* Tuojiangosaurus.

LEFT Kentrosaurus *was well defended against predators such as the formidable* Ceratosaurus.

BELOW *The incredible armour of the mighty* Ankylosaurus.

51

SPIKY LIZARD

Kentrosaurus ("spiked lizard") was an African cousin to the larger and better-known *Stegosaurus*. Pairs of bony plates protected its neck, shoulders and back, while a double row of long, sharp spikes covered its lower back and tail. A further pair of spikes jutted out from this dinosaur's shoulders, providing defence from predators such as the fearsome *Ceratosaurus*.

❧ EUOPLOCEPHALUS ❧

One of the best-known armoured dinosaurs is the late-Cretaceous *Euoplocephalus*. Roughly the size of a small elephant, this creature was covered in spikes and bony plates, while its tail ended in a heavy, bone-crushing club. Predators such as *Gorgosaurus* would have had great difficulty in reaching the soft flesh of its belly.

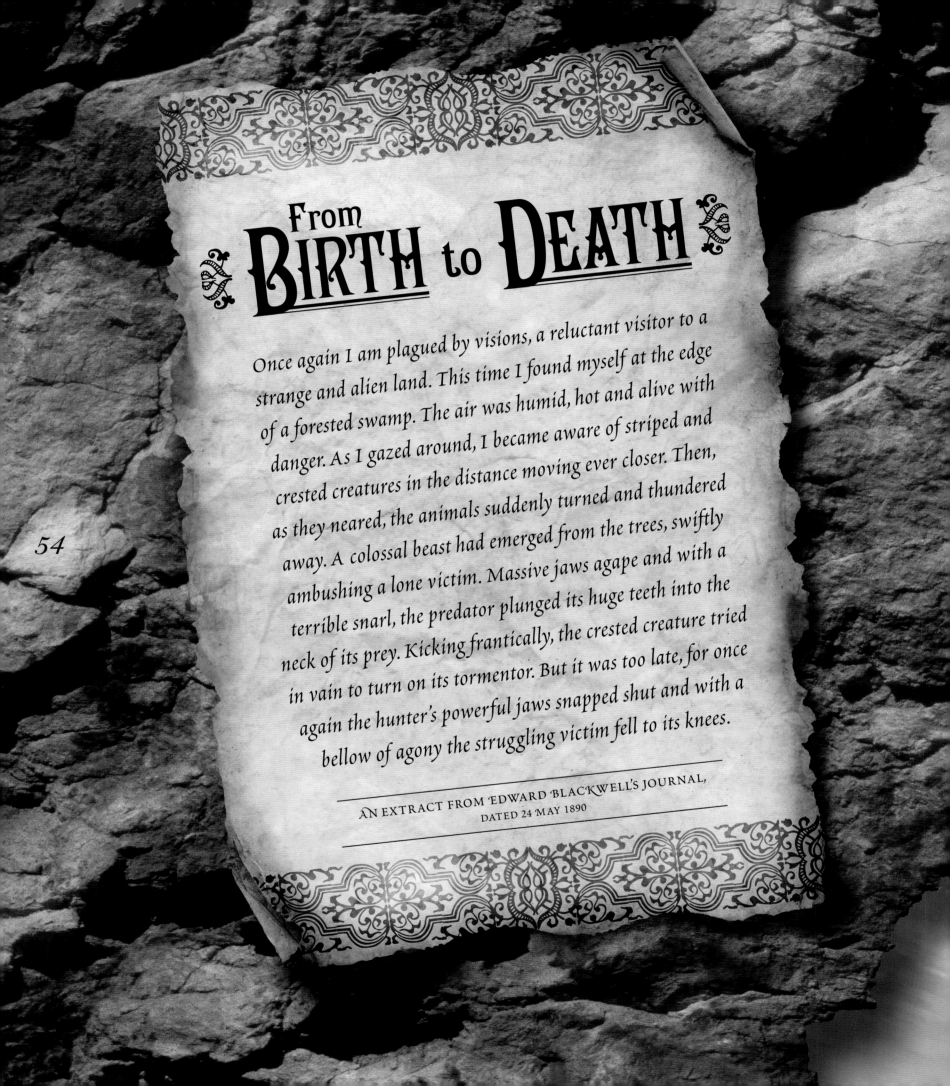

From BIRTH to DEATH

Once again I am plagued by visions, a reluctant visitor to a strange and alien land. This time I found myself at the edge of a forested swamp. The air was humid, hot and alive with danger. As I gazed around, I became aware of striped and crested creatures in the distance moving ever closer. Then, as they neared, the animals suddenly turned and thundered away. A colossal beast had emerged from the trees, swiftly ambushing a lone victim. Massive jaws agape and with a terrible snarl, the predator plunged its huge teeth into the neck of its prey. Kicking frantically, the crested creature tried in vain to turn on its tormentor. But it was too late, for once again the hunter's powerful jaws snapped shut and with a bellow of agony the struggling victim fell to its knees.

AN EXTRACT FROM EDWARD BLACKWELL'S JOURNAL,
DATED 24 MAY 1890

EGGS and NESTS

DINOSAURS hatched from hard-shelled eggs, just as birds do today. Egg fossils have been found across the world – incredibly a few have even contained the bones of unborn babies. Small dinosaurs probably sat on their eggs to keep them warm, while larger dinosaurs may have buried their eggs, or relied on the sun and rotting vegetation placed in the nest to incubate them. Some newly hatched dinosaurs were cared for by their parents, while others had to fend for themselves from the moment they emerged.

EGGS OF A GIANT

Dinosaur eggs came in many shapes and sizes – some were large and round, perhaps the size of a football, while others were long and narrow like a loaf of bread. The smallest eggs could fit in the palm of a human hand. The sauropods typically laid cannonball-shaped eggs, around 13 cm across. It is incredible to think that the dinosaurs that hatched from these eggs grew to such enormous sizes. However, larger eggs would have needed much thicker shells, and the hatchlings would not have been able to crack through them.

LEFT *A baby dinosaur hatches from its egg.*

LEFT *A group of hadrosaur eggs from the Jurassic period.*

DINOSAUR NURSERIES

Most dinosaurs built nests, either scraping a hole in the ground or building a muddy rim to encircle the eggs. The discovery of many nests in single sites shows that some dinosaurs laid eggs in colonies for protection from predators. *Maiasaura* ("good mother lizard") was a large duck-billed dinosaur that lived in the late Cretaceous period. Many mud nests have been discovered side by side in Montana, USA, one even holding the remains of babies too large to be hatchlings. This suggests that *Maiasaura* cared for its young until they were large enough to fend for themselves.

57

ABOVE Maiasaura protected its eggs from predators.

BELOW *Many dinosaurs laid their eggs in a hole scraped in the ground.*

❧ MUTTABURRASAURUS ❧

The large bulge on the snout of
Muttaburrasaurus ("Muttaburra lizard")
may have been used to make loud, honking
noises. It is likely that this dinosaur roamed
in herds and probably used these sounds to
communicate with other members of its group.

~ HERDS ~

Tracks of many dinosaurs found together and huge "bone beds" with large numbers of fossils from the same species reveal that some plant-eating dinosaurs lived in herds for protection. Like modern-day buffaloes or birds, herds of dinosaurs may have travelled huge distances every year, returning to the same sites for warmth and food.

Dinosaur Graveyard

In 2010, scientists announced the discovery of the largest known dinosaur bone bed in Alberta, Canada. The thousands of jumbled bones are the remains of the late-Cretaceous horned dinosaur *Centrosaurus* ("pointed lizard"). Scientists believe that these dinosaurs were killed by a catastrophic storm. Although bone beds with fossils from this species have been found in the past, the sheer size of this new site reveals that these and other horned dinosaurs very likely lived in herds numbering thousands.

Cretaceous Cattle

The hadrosaurs or duck-billed dinosaurs have been called the "cows of the Cretaceous". They were extremely common and roamed in giant herds, constantly stripping and grinding vegetation. Living in a herd creates a barrier to hungry predators. At the first sign of danger these dinosaurs probably made loud bellowing noises to alert the rest of the herd. This would have been helpful as the hadrosaurs had few defences against attack.

INTELLIGENCE

Dinosaurs have long had a reputation for stupidity. One of the earliest dinosaurs to be discovered and named, the truck-sized *Stegosaurus*, had a brain where the thinking part – the cerebellum – was the size of a walnut!

Intelligence Stakes

However, it is clear that some dinosaurs had more brainpower than others. The least intelligent dinosaurs were the sauropods whose brains were tiny compared to their enormous bodies. The hadrosaurs had bigger brains and were probably more intelligent than other plant-eaters – living in herds, these dinosaurs had more complex social lives. The flesh-eaters needed sharper senses to seek out and capture their prey, and were the most intelligent of all.

A Quick-Witted Hunter

Troodon ("wounding tooth") had the heaviest brain compared to its body size, and was perhaps the smartest dinosaur of all. This small and agile hunter of the late Cretaceous period had large, forward-facing eyes, meaning it could accurately judge distances, as well as heightened senses of smell and hearing. These advantages helped *Troodon* to stalk and capture its prey. However, despite having more intelligence than almost all other dinosaurs, *Troodon* was only about as bright as the modern-day ostrich – and less intelligent than most mammals living today.

❦ TROODON ❧

*Troodon*s prepare to feast on the giant corpse of a titanosaur. Although a quick-witted hunter, *Troodon* was probably a scavenger too, feeding on larger prey when the opportunity arose.

PACK HUNTERS

Like a pack of hungry wolves, some flesh-eating dinosaurs may have banded together and hunted in groups. Armed with vicious claws and powerful jaws, these hunters would have used stealth and cunning — and sheer weight of numbers — to overwhelm larger and more powerful prey.

ABOVE *This skeleton of* Deinonychus *shows its lethal weapons of blade-like teeth and hooked talons.*

RIGHT *A Deinonychus* claw fossil.

Swift Killers

Several near-complete *Deinonychus* fossils found near the remains of the plant-eater *Tenontosaurus* have led some scientists to speculate that this fast and ferocious predator hunted in packs. Perhaps *Deinonychus* and other related dinosaurs such as *Velociraptor* and *Utahraptor* used teamwork to silently encircle their prey. Cutting off all routes of escape, they could then move in for the kill using their massive, hooked claws and blade-like fangs to end their victim's life. Devouring their feast, these bloodthirsty hunters would have squabbled over the remains as they quickly stripped the corpse, reducing it to a bare skeleton.

LEFT *A ferocious* Deinonychus *pack closes in on a* Tenontosaurus.

TREE BROWSERS

Plants are much more difficult for an animal to process than meat, as tough vegetation needs to be broken down for digestion. Plant-eating dinosaurs dealt with this problem in a variety of ways.

PLANT PROCESSORS

The blunt teeth of the large sauropods were no good for chewing – instead twigs and leaves were swallowed whole or partially broken up. Plant material was then slowly processed in the sauropods' enormous guts. The hadrosaurs had tough beaks for pulling in vegetation and hundreds of tiny grinding teeth arranged in groups. The horned dinosaurs used their sharp, parrot-like beaks for slicing through tough plants that were then ground to a pulp with scissor-sharp teeth.

BIG EATERS

A massive sauropod like *Brachiosaurus* ("arm lizard") would have needed to consume vast quantities just to stay alive. Not having to chew its food meant this dinosaur could spend all its time eating – browsing the treetops, it shovelled in vegetation using its spoon-shaped teeth to break off tough leaves. Many scientists have tried to explain why the sauropods became so enormous. One possible reason is that being large gave them protection from the big meat-eaters. But it seems these predators responded by becoming even larger, driving the sauropods to truly colossal sizes.

❧ BRACHIOSAURUS ❧

Brachiosaurus could reach as high as 15 m up into the trees to feed. With its massive front legs and immensely long neck, it was perhaps able to stretch higher than any other dinosaur.

❧ TRICERATOPS ❧

The mighty *Triceratops* had a huge head, an extraordinary neck frill, two long brow horns and a short nose horn. Injuries preserved on fossils reveal that rival males very likely fought with each other, as shown here, in a bid to win a mate or territory. The horns were almost certainly used in self-defence too, against predators such as *Tyrannosaurus rex*.

FEROCIOUS KILLERS

THE meat-eaters or theropods ("beast-footed") included the largest predators ever to stalk the Earth. These terrifying killers had strangely short arms, but powerfully muscled rear legs and massive, deadly jaws. However, as we have already seen, not all the meat-eaters were huge and heavily built. The vicious *Utahraptor* ("Utah's predator") was a lightly built hunter the size of a grizzly bear, while the insect-snatching *Mei long* ("sleeping dragon") was no bigger than a duck.

ABOVE *Each foot of* Tyrannosaurus rex *had three fearsome claws on forward-pointing toes. A small and harmless fourth claw was set off to the side.*

BELOW Utahraptor *had jaws lined with viciously sharp teeth.*

TYRANT KING

The most famous — and feared — carnivore the world has ever seen, *Tyrannosaurus rex* was 12 m long, 5 m high and weighed around 6 tonnes. This monster had immensely powerful jaws and would have had no trouble in gulping down a human whole.

Tyrannosaurus rex had tiny arms relative to its size — some scientists suggest that they were too short to hold on to its prey and that this dinosaur was in fact a scavenger, feeding on animals that were already dead. However, most scientists believe that, like the modern-day lion, *Tyrannosaurus rex* was a fearsome hunter that scavenged when the opportunity arose.

LEFT *Giganotosaurus, even larger than* Tyrannosaurus rex, *stalked its prey with grasping, clawed hands and enormous fanged jaws.*

MIGHTY HUNTERS

Although *Tyrannosaurus rex* is by far the best-known predatory dinosaur, other meat-eaters were bigger still. *Giganotosaurus* ("giant southern lizard") lived in South America during the Cretaceous period, and was larger and heavier than *Tyrannosaurus rex*, though its brain was smaller and its jaws less powerful. The late-Cretaceous *Spinosaurus* may have been the largest theropod of all. Its length has been estimated at around 16 m and the strange "fin" on its back grew to at least 1.6 m in height. This giant's jaws and teeth were suited to hunting fish, though it was probably powerful enough to have preyed on medium-sized dinosaurs too.

CROCODILE JAWS

Baryonyx ("heavy claw") was an early-Cretaceous dinosaur, first discovered in England. It had a long crocodile-like snout and finely serrated teeth perfect for gripping large, slippery fish. *Baryonyx* was named for the huge claw on the thumb of each hand – this weapon was probably used to hook and scoop its prey from the water.

BELOW *The enormous hooked thumb-claws of* **Baryonyx.**

⚜ TYRANNOSAURUS REX ⚜

Tyrannosaurus rex clamps its massive jaws round the neck of a struggling *Hypacrosaurus*. This predator's incredible bite was more powerful than that of any other dinosaur, or indeed any land animal to walk the Earth before or since.

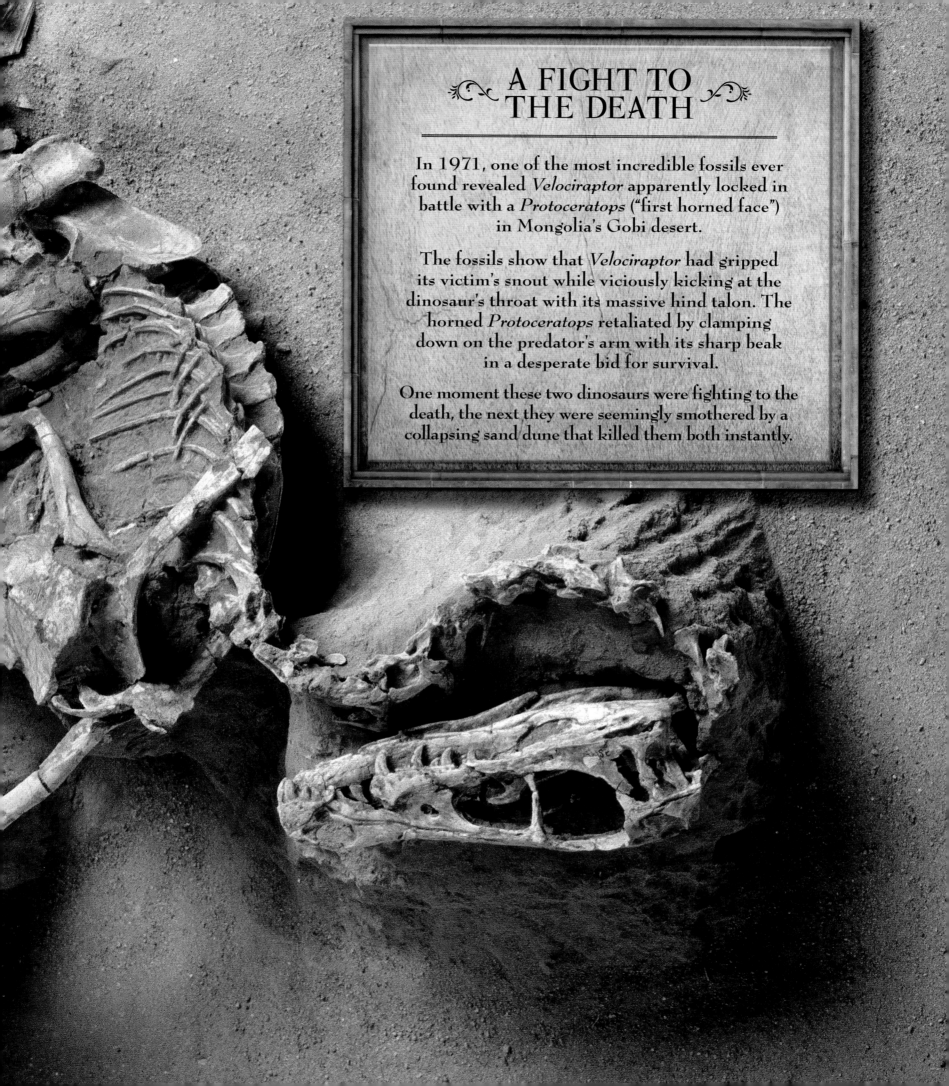

A FIGHT TO THE DEATH

In 1971, one of the most incredible fossils ever found revealed *Velociraptor* apparently locked in battle with a *Protoceratops* ("first horned face") in Mongolia's Gobi desert.

The fossils show that *Velociraptor* had gripped its victim's snout while viciously kicking at the dinosaur's throat with its massive hind talon. The horned *Protoceratops* retaliated by clamping down on the predator's arm with its sharp beak in a desperate bid for survival.

One moment these two dinosaurs were fighting to the death, the next they were seemingly smothered by a collapsing sand dune that killed them both instantly.

DEATH and EXTINCTION

The dinosaurs prospered for over 160 million years. Then, 65 million years ago, they all suddenly vanished apart from the small, feathered theropods we now know as birds. More than half of all species on Earth perished alongside the dinosaurs, including large sea reptiles and the pterosaurs. What catastrophic event could have had such disastrous consequences?

Fatal Collision

Most scientists are now agreed that a massive impact from space caused the mass extinction. An asteroid or space rock, 10–15 km wide, smashed into Earth at Chicxulub on Mexico's Yucatan Peninsula. It is estimated that the resulting explosion was a billion times more powerful than a nuclear bomb. The impact would have caused huge fires, massive earthquakes, volcanoes and tsunamis. Clouds of dust would have blocked out the sun for months, shrouding the planet in darkness and causing a worldwide winter. The dinosaurs simply could not adapt to such terrible conditions – their long reign was over.

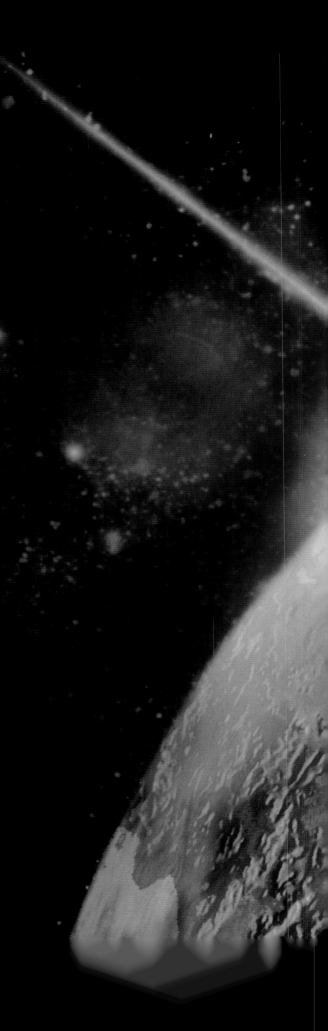

MYSTERY AT HELL CREEK

PALAEONTOLOGISTS excavating the fossilized remains of a *Tyrannosaurus rex* at the Hell Creek formation in Montana have made a grisly find. Scattered human bones were discovered by a member of the team close to the site of the current dig.

The remains were at first thought to be those of a wild animal, but when it became clear they were human, the police and a pathologist were called in to investigate. Only a few bones have been recovered, but an initial examination suggests they are those of a male adult between 30 and 40 years old who died over 100 years ago.

Investigators also recovered a nineteenth-century rock hammer from the vicinity, which may have belonged to the individual. Extremely weathered, it appears to be inscribed with the initials EAD or EAB. However, as Hell Creek has been the site of numerous digs, it is impossible to be sure of its owner.

Dr Joanna Stevens, who was leading the dig, spoke of her shock at the chance find. "We came here to dig out the remains of 70-million-year-old dinosaur – we didn't expect to find human remains. It certainly is an intriguing mystery."

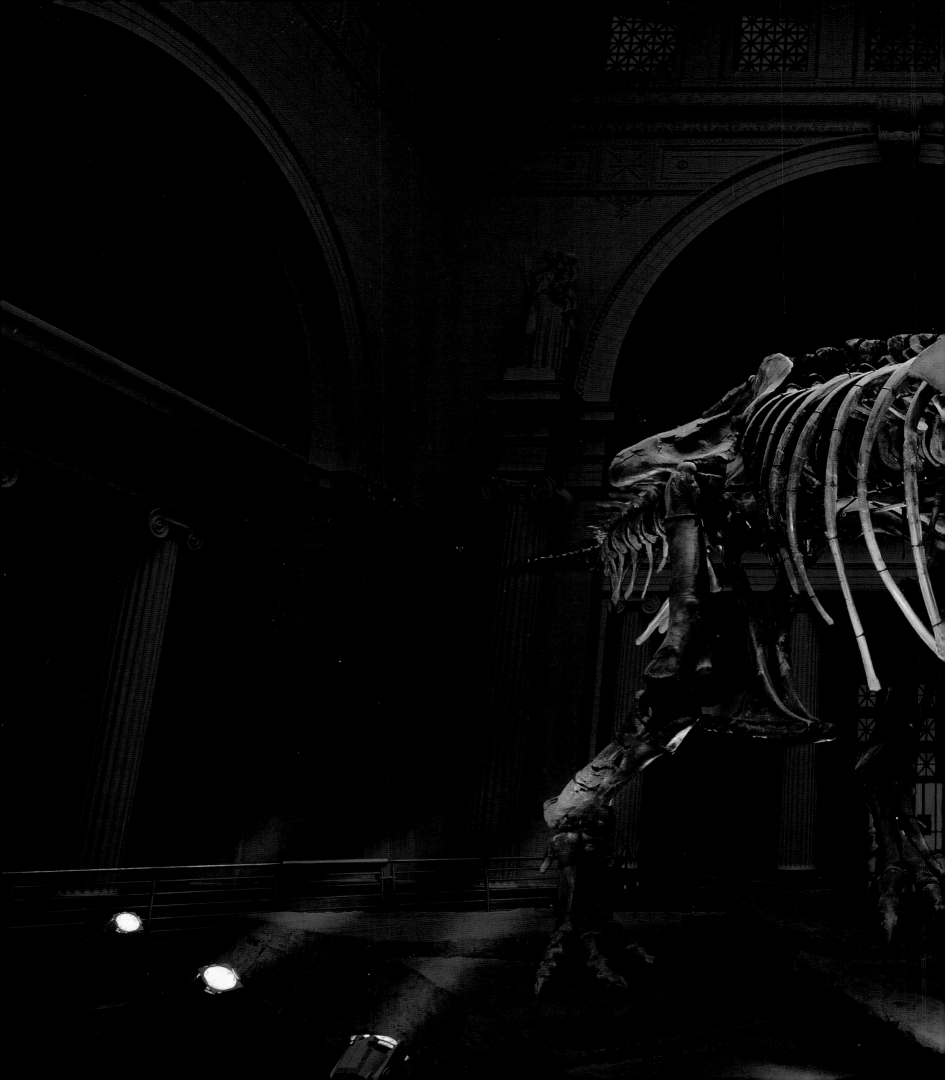

ACKNOWLEDGEMENTS

My sincere thanks and appreciation must be extended to the following individuals, without whose assistance this book could not have been completed:

To several of my relatives - especially Arthur and Jean Blackwell, James and Emma Blackwell, Sandra Caldwell and Laura Doulton - for sharing their memories and knowledge in my quest to piece together Edward Blackwell's story; the palaeontologist Darren Naish, for his rigorous checking of the facts and helpful suggestions; my editor Barry Timms for his invaluable pointers; Russell Porter, Clare Baggaley, Ceri Hurst and Alison Tutton for the superb book design; Drew McGovern for his skilled Photoshop work; Andrew Kerr for the astonishingly life-like artworks; Stuart Martin for the wonderful pencil drawings; Ben White for excellent picture research; and Kate Pimm for the fine production.

Finally, I would like to pay tribute to my great grandfather, the late Edward Blackwell, whose writings first inspired me and whose remarkable story gripped my imagination. Without him and his passion for dinosaurs, this book would not exist.

Archie Blackwell

80

This is a Carlton book

Text, design and illustration
© Carlton Books Limited 2011

CARLTON
BOOKS

Published in 2011 by Carlton Books Limited
An imprint of the Carlton Publishing Group
20 Mortimer Street, London W1T 3JW

10 9 8 7 6 5 4 3 2 1

All rights reserved. This book is sold subject to the condition that it may not be reproduced, stored in a retrieval system or transmitted in any form or by any means, electronic, mechanical, photocopying, recording or otherwise, without the publisher's prior consent.

The views contained herein are those of the author and do not necessarily reflect those of the publisher.

A catalogue record for this book is available from the British Library.

ISBN: 978-1-84732-861-8

Printed in Dongguan, China

PICTURE CREDITS

The publishers would like to thank the following sources for their kind permission to reproduce the pictures in this book.

AMNH: 24l, 76, 32-33

Alamy Images: /Leonello Calvetti: 69t, /Phil Degginger/Carnegie Museum: 17t, /Eddie Gerald: 76-77, /Leslie Garland Picture Library: 44 br, /Nancy G Stock Photography: 38-39, /Alex Ramsay: 68tr, /Lana Sundman: 40l, 62tr, 40-41,

Corbis: /Sanford/Agliolo: 74-75, /Jonathan Blair: 16, /DK Limited: 35br, 69br, /Walter Geiersperger: 40tl, /Chris Hellier: 29bl, /Jean-Baptiste Rabouan/Hemis: 78-79, /Louie Psihoyos: 24b, 42, 43, 44tl, /Louis Psihoyos: 5t, 72-73, /Kimimasa Mayama/Reuters: 68bl, /Visuals Unlimited: 21b, 34-35t

Getty Images: 45r, /Dorling Kindersley: 37br, /Colin Keates: 37t, /National Geographic: 51, /Louie Psihoyos: 20b, 29br, 44c, /Science & Society Picture Library: 25

istockphoto.com: 5tr, 5r, 5b, 9tl

Natural History Museum: 29tl, 35tl, 37l, 44bl, 45bl, 34-35b, 46-49, /Anness Publishing Ltd: 35tr

Photolibrary.com: 12-13, /Peter Arnold Images: 21t

Private Collection: 28

Science Photo Library: 13bl, /Carlos Goldin: 44b, /Ted Kinsman: 20t, /Martin Sheilds: 21r, /Sinclair Stammers: 56-57

Stock.XCHNG: 4c

thinkstockphotos.com: 4bl, 12, 13bl, 17br, 41, 22-23

Topfoto.co.uk: /Granger Collection: 13r, /National Pictures: 9b

Yale University: 62l

Every effort has been made to acknowledge correctly and contact the source and/or copyright holder of each picture and Carlton Books Limited apologises for any unintentional errors or omissions which will be corrected in future editions of this book.